THE LITTLE LIBRARY OF EARTH MEDICINE

SNAKE

Kenneth Meadows

Illustrations by Jo Donegan

DK PUBLISHING, INC.

A DK PUBLISHING BOOK

The Little Library of Earth Medicine was
produced, edited, and designed by
GLS Editorial and Design
Garden Studios, 11-15 Betterton Street
London WC2H 9BP

Editorial director: Jane Laing
Design director: Ruth Shane
Project designer: Luke Herriott
Editors: Claire Calman, Terry Burrows, Victoria Sorzano
US Editors: Jennifer Dorr, William Lach, Barbara Minton

Additional illustrations: Roy Flooks 16, 17, 31; John Lawrence 38
Special photography: Mark Hamilton
Picture credits: American Natural History Museum 8-9, 12, 14-15, 32

First American Edition, 1998
2 4 6 8 10 9 7 5 3 1

Published in the United States by DK Publishing, Inc.
95 Madison Avenue, New York, NY 10016
Visit us on the World Wide Web at http://www.dk.com.

Library of Congress Cataloging-in-Publication Data
Meadows, Kenneth.
   The little library of earth medicine / by Kenneth Meadows. – 1st American ed.
      p.   cm.
      Contents: |1| Falcon, 21st March-19th April – |2| Beaver, 20th April-20 May – |3|
Deer, 21st May-20th June – |4| Woodpecker, 21st June-21st July – |5| Salmon, 22nd July-
21st August – |6| Brown Bear, 22nd August-21st September – |7| Crow, 22nd
September-22nd October – |8| Snake, 23rd October-22nd November – |9| Owl, 23rd
November-21st December – |10| Goose, 22nd December-19 January – |11| Otter, 20th
January-18th February – |12| Wolf, 19th February-20th March.
      Includes indexes.
      ISBN 0-7894-2879-2
      1. Medicine wheels–Miscellanea. 2. Horoscopes. 3. Indians of North
America–Religion–Miscellanea. 4. Typology (Psychology)–Miscellanea. I. Title.
BF1623.M43M42 1998
133.5'9397–dc21   97-42267
                                                                                  CIP

Reproduced by Kestrel Digital Colour Ltd, Chelmsford, Essex
Printed and bound in Hong Kong by Imago

CONTENTS

INTRODUCING
EARTH MEDICINE

TO NATIVE AMERICANS, MEDICINE IS NOT AN EXTERNAL SUBSTANCE BUT AN INNER POWER THAT IS FOUND IN BOTH NATURE AND OURSELVES.

Earth Medicine is a unique method of personality profiling that draws on Native American under-standing of the Universe, and on the principles embodied in sacred Medicine Wheels.

Native Americans believed that spirit, although invisible, permeated Nature, so that everything in Nature was sacred. Animals were perceived as acting as

Shaman's rattle
Shamans used rattles to connect with their inner spirit. This is a Tlingit shaman's wooden rattle.

messengers of spirit. They also appeared in waking dreams to impart power known as "medicine." The recipients of such dreams honored the animal species that appeared to them by rendering their images on ceremonial, ornamental, and everyday artifacts.

NATURE WITHIN SELF
Native American shamans – tribal wisemen – recognized similarities between the natural forces prevalent during the seasons and the characteristics of those born

"Spirit has provided you with an opportunity to study in Nature's university." **Stoney teaching**

during corresponding times of the year. They also noted how personality is affected by the four phases of the Moon – at birth and throughout life – and by the continual alternation of energy flow, from active to passive. This view is encapsulated in Earth Medicine, which helps you to recognize how the dynamics of Nature function within you and how the potential strengths you were born with can be developed.

MEDICINE WHEELS

Native American cultural traditions embrace a variety of circular symbolic images and objects. These sacred hoops have become known as Medicine

Animal ornament

To the Anasazi, who carved this ornament from jet, the frog symbolized adaptability.

Wheels, due to their similarity to the spoked wheels of the wagons that carried settlers into the heartlands of once-Native American territory. Each Medicine Wheel showed how different objects or qualities related to one another within the context of a greater whole, and how different forces and energies moved within it.

One Medicine Wheel might be regarded as the master wheel because it indicated balance within Nature and the most effective way of achieving harmony with the Universe and ourselves. It is upon this master Medicine Wheel (see pp.10–11) that Earth Medicine is structured.

Feast dish

Stylized bear carvings adorn this Tlingit feast dish. To the Native American, the bear symbolizes strength and self-sufficiency.

THE MEDICINE WHEEL

The outer Wheel is divided into twelve birth times, each of which has its own animal totem, and stone, tree, and color affinities.

At the hub of the Wheel, surrounded by representations of Elements, Directions, and energy flow, is the Wakan-Tanka — symbol of invisible energies coming into physical reality.

Season of birth
Each of the twelve segments relates to a specific time of year (see pp.12–13).

NORTH: WINTER

WEST: AUTUMN

WOLF

OTTER

GOOSE

OWL

SNAKE

CROW

Wakan-Tanka
The powerful symbol used by some Native Americans to denote energy coming into form (see p.24).

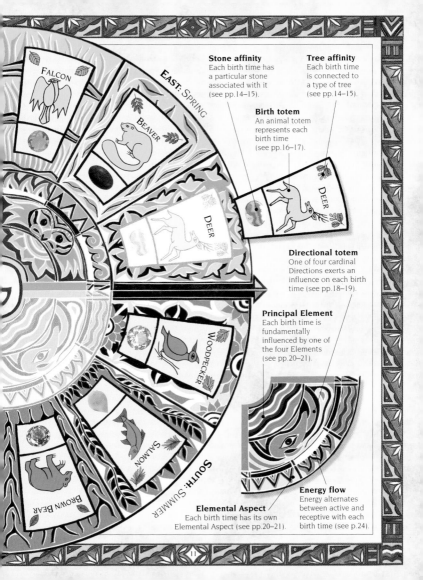

Stone affinity
Each birth time has a particular stone associated with it (see pp.14–15).

Tree affinity
Each birth time is connected to a type of tree (see pp.14–15).

Birth totem
An animal totem represents each birth time (see pp.16–17).

Directional totem
One of four cardinal Directions exerts an influence on each birth time (see pp.18–19).

Principal Element
Each birth time is fundamentally influenced by one of the four Elements (see pp.20–21).

Energy flow
Energy alternates between active and receptive with each birth time (see p.24).

Elemental Aspect
Each birth time has its own Elemental Aspect (see pp.20–21).

EAST: SPRING

SOUTH: SUMMER

FALCON

BEAVER

DEER

DEER

WOODPECKER

SALMON

BROWN BEAR

THE TWELVE
BIRTH TIMES

THE STRUCTURE OF THE MEDICINE WHEEL IS BASED UPON THE SEASONS TO REFLECT THE POWERFUL INFLUENCE OF NATURE ON HUMAN PERSONALITY.

The Medicine Wheel classifies human nature into twelve personality types, each corresponding to the characteristics of Nature at a particular time of the year. It is designed to act as a kind of map to help you discover your strengths and weaknesses, your inner drives and instinctive behaviors, and your true potential.

The four seasons form the basis of the Wheel's structure, with the Summer and Winter solstices and the Spring and Autumn equinoxes marking each season's passing. In Earth Medicine,

Seasonal rites

Performers at the Iroquois mid-Winter ceremony wore masks made of braided maize husks. They danced to attune themselves to energies that would ensure a good harvest.

each season is a metaphor for a stage of human growth and development. Spring is likened to infancy and the newness of life, and Summer to the exuberance of youth and of rapid development. Autumn represents the fulfillment that mature adulthood brings, while Winter symbolizes the accumulated wisdom that can be drawn upon in later life.

Each seasonal quarter of the Wheel is further divided into three periods, making twelve time segments altogether. The time of your birth determines the direction from which

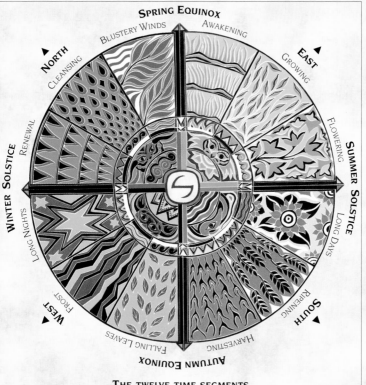

THE TWELVE TIME SEGMENTS

(wheel labels, clockwise from top)

SPRING EQUINOX

BLUSTERY WINDS · AWAKENING

NORTH ▲

CLEANSING · GROWING · EAST ▲

RENEWAL · FLOWERING

WINTER SOLSTICE · SUMMER SOLSTICE

LONG NIGHTS · LONG DAYS

WEST ▲ · RIPENING

FROST · SOUTH ▲

FALLING LEAVES · HARVESTING

AUTUMN EQUINOX

you perceive life, and the qualities imbued in Nature in that season are reflected in your core character.

Each of the twelve time segments, or birth times, is named after a feature in the natural yearly cycle. For example, the period after the Spring equinox is called Awakening time because it is the time of new growth, while the segment after the Autumn equinox is named after the falling leaves that characterize that time.

THE SIGNIFICANCE OF
TOTEMS

NATIVE AMERICANS BELIEVED THAT TOTEMS — ANIMAL SYMBOLS — REPRESENTED ESSENTIAL TRUTHS AND ACTED AS CONNECTIONS TO NATURAL POWERS.

 totem is an animal or natural object adopted as an emblem to typify certain distinctive qualities. Native Americans regarded animals, whose behavior is predictable, as particularly useful guides to categorizing human patterns of behavior.

A totem mirrors aspects of your nature and unlocks the intuitive knowledge that lies beyond the reasoning capacity of the intellect. It may take the form of a carving or molding, a pictorial image, or a token of fur, feather, bone, tooth, or claw. Its presence serves as an immediate link with the energies it represents. A totem is therefore more effective than a glyph or symbol as an aid to comprehending nonphysical powers and formative forces.

PRIMARY TOTEMS

In Earth Medicine you have three primary totems: a birth totem, a Directional totem, and an Elemental totem. Your *birth totem* is the embodiment of core characteristics that correspond with the dominant aspects of Nature during your birth time.

Symbol of strength
The handle of this Tlingit knife is carved with a raven and a bear head, symbols of insight and inner strength.

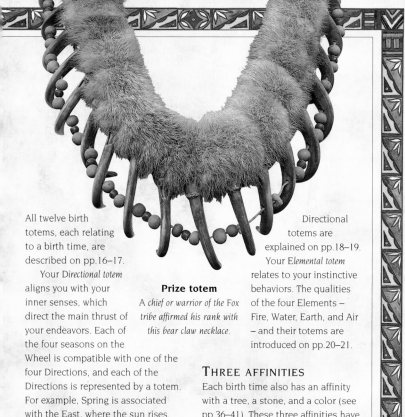

All twelve birth totems, each relating to a birth time, are described on pp.16–17.

Your *Directional totem* aligns you with your inner senses, which direct the main thrust of your endeavors. Each of the four seasons on the Wheel is compatible with one of the four Directions, and each of the Directions is represented by a totem. For example, Spring is associated with the East, where the sun rises, and signifies seeing things in new ways; its totem is the Eagle. The four

Prize totem

A chief or warrior of the Fox tribe affirmed his rank with this bear claw necklace.

Directional totems are explained on pp.18–19.

Your E*lemental totem* relates to your instinctive behaviors. The qualities of the four Elements – Fire, Water, Earth, and Air – and their totems are introduced on pp.20–21.

THREE AFFINITIES

Each birth time also has an affinity with a tree, a stone, and a color (see pp.36–41). These three affinities have qualities that can strengthen you during challenging times.

"If a man is to succeed, he must be governed not by his inclination, but by an understanding of the ways of animals..." Teton Sioux teaching

THE TWELVE
BIRTH TOTEMS

THE TWELVE BIRTH TIMES ARE REPRESENTED BY TOTEMS,
EACH ONE AN ANIMAL THAT BEST EXPRESSES THE
QUALITIES INHERENT IN THAT BIRTH TIME.

Earth Medicine associates an animal totem with each birth time (the two sets of dates below reflect the difference in season between the Northern and Southern Hemispheres). These animals help to connect you to the powers and abilities that they represent. For an in-depth study of the Snake birth totem, see pp.28–29.

FALCON
March 21–April 19 (N. Hem)
Sept 22–Oct 22 (S. Hem)
Falcons are full of initiative, but often rush in to make decisions they may later regret. Lively and extroverted, they have enthusiasm for new experiences but can sometimes lack persistence.

DEER
May 21–June 20 (N. Hem)
Nov 23–Dec 21 (S. Hem)
Deer are willing to sacrifice the old for the new. They loathe routine, thriving on variety and challenges. They have a wild side, often leaping from one situation or relationship into another without reflection.

BEAVER
April 20–May 20 (N. Hem)
Oct 23–Nov 22 (S. Hem)
Practical and steady, Beavers have a capacity for perseverance. Good homemakers, they are warm and affectionate but need harmony and peace to avoid becoming irritable. They have a keen aesthetic sense.

WOODPECKER
June 21–July 21 (N. Hem)
Dec 22–Jan 19 (S. Hem)
Emotional and sensitive, Woodpeckers are warm to those closest to them, and willing to sacrifice their needs for those of their loved ones. They have lively imaginations but can be worriers.

SALMON
July 22 – August 21 (N. Hem)
Jan 20 – Feb 18 (S. Hem)

Enthusiastic and self-confident, Salmon people enjoy running things. They are uncompromising and forceful, and can occasionally seem a little arrogant or self-important. They are easily hurt by neglect.

OWL
Nov 23 – Dec 21 (N. Hem)
May 21 – June 20 (S. Hem)

Owls need freedom of expression. They are lively, self-reliant, and have an eye for detail. Inquisitive and adaptable, they have a tendency to overextend themselves. Owls are often physically courageous.

BROWN BEAR
August 22 – Sept 21 (N. Hem)
Feb 19 – March 20 (S. Hem)

Brown Bears are hardworking, practical, and self-reliant. They do not like change, preferring to stick to what is familiar. They have a flair for fixing things, are good-natured, and make good friends.

GOOSE
Dec 22 – Jan 19 (N. Hem)
June 21 – July 21 (S. Hem)

Goose people are far-sighted idealists who are willing to explore the unknown. They approach life with enthusiasm, determined to fulfill their dreams. They are perfectionists, and can appear unduly serious.

CROW
Sept 22 – Oct 22 (N. Hem)
March 21 – April 19 (S. Hem)

Crows dislike solitude and feel most comfortable in company. Although usually pleasant and good-natured, they can be strongly influenced by negative atmospheres, becoming gloomy and prickly.

OTTER
Jan 20 – Feb 18 (N. Hem)
July 22 – August 21 (S. Hem)

Otters are friendly, lively, and perceptive. They feel inhibited by too many rules and regulations, which often makes them appear eccentric. They like cleanliness and order, and have original minds.

SNAKE
Oct 23 – Nov 22 (N. Hem)
April 20 – May 20 (S. Hem)

Snakes are secretive and mysterious, hiding their feelings beneath a cool exterior. Adaptable, determined, and imaginative, they are capable of bouncing back from tough situations encountered in life.

WOLF
Feb 19 – March 20 (N. Hem)
August 22 – Sept 21 (S. Hem)

Wolves are sensitive, artistic, and intuitive – people to whom others turn for help. They value freedom and their own space, and are easily affected by others. They are philosophical, trusting, and genuine.

THE INFLUENCE OF THE
DIRECTIONS

ALSO KNOWN BY NATIVE AMERICANS AS THE FOUR
WINDS, THE INFLUENCE OF THE FOUR DIRECTIONS IS
EXPERIENCED THROUGH YOUR INNER SENSES.

Regarded as the "keepers" or "caretakers" of the Universe, the four Directions or alignments were also referred to by Native Americans as the four Winds because their presence was felt rather than seen.

DIRECTIONAL TOTEMS
In Earth Medicine, each Direction or Wind is associated with a season and a time of day. Thus the Autumn birth times – Falling Leaves time, Frost time, and Long Nights time –

all fall within the West Direction, and evening. The Direction to which your birth time belongs influences the nature of your inner senses.

The East Direction is associated with illumination. Its totem is the Eagle – a bird that soars closest to the Sun and can see clearly from height. The South is the Direction of Summer and the afternoon. It signifies growth and fruition, fluidity, and emotions. Its totem, the Mouse, symbolizes productivity, feelings, and an ability to perceive detail.

"Remember...the circle of the sky, the stars, the super-natural Winds breathing night and day...the four Directions." Pawnee teaching

The four Directions

*Each Direction is associated with a
season and a time of day, and also
with a principal function: the East
with determining, the South with
giving, the West with holding, and
the North with receiving.*

SPRING EQUINOX

NORTH

EAST

BUFFALO

EAGLE

WINTER SOLSTICE

SUMMER SOLSTICE

GRIZZLY BEAR

MOUSE

WEST

SOUTH

AUTUMN EQUINOX

The West is the Direction of Autumn
and the evening. It signifies
transformation – from day to night,
from Summer to Winter – and the
qualities of introspection and
conservation. Its totem is the Grizzly
Bear, which represents strength

drawn from within. The North is the
Direction of Winter and the night,
and is associated with the mind and
its sustenance – knowledge. Its
totem is the Buffalo, an animal that
was honored by Native Americans as
the great material "provider."

THE INFLUENCE OF THE ELEMENTS

THE FOUR ELEMENTS — AIR, FIRE, WATER, AND EARTH — PERVADE EVERYTHING AND INDICATE THE NATURE OF MOVEMENT AND THE ESSENCE OF WHO YOU ARE.

E lements are intangible qualities that describe the essential state or character of all things. In Earth Medicine, the four Elements are allied with four fundamental modes of activity and are associated with different aspects of the self. Air expresses free movement in all directions; it is related to the mind and to thinking. Fire indicates expansive motion; it is linked with the spirit and with intuition. Water signifies fluidity; it

Elemental profile
The configuration of Snake is Water of Earth. Earth is the Principal Element and Water the Elemental Aspect.

has associations with the soul and the emotions. Earth symbolizes stability; it is related to the physical body and the sensations.

ELEMENTAL DISTRIBUTION

On the Medicine Wheel one Element is associated with each of the four Directions – Fire in the East, Earth in the West, Air in the North, and Water in the South. These are known as the Principal Elements.

The four Elements also have an individual association with each of the twelve birth times – known as the Elemental Aspects. They follow a cyclical sequence around the Wheel based on the action of the Sun (Fire) on the Earth, producing atmosphere (Air) and condensation (Water).

The three birth times that share an Elemental Aspect belong to the same Elemental family or "clan," with a totem that gives insight into its key characteristics. Snake people belong to the Frog clan (see pp.34–35).

ELEMENTAL EMPHASIS

For each birth time, the qualities of the Elemental Aspect usually predominate over those of the Principal Element, although both are present to give a specific configuration, such as Fire of Earth (for Snake's, see pp.34–35). For Falcon, Woodpecker, and Otter, the Principal Element and the Elemental Aspect are identical (for example, Air of Air), so people of these totems tend to express that Element intensely.

AIR

WATER

FIRE

EARTH

EARTH

AIR

THE INFLUENCE OF THE
MOON

THE WAXING AND WANING OF THE MOON DURING ITS
FOUR PHASES HAS A CRUCIAL INFLUENCE ON THE
FORMATION OF PERSONALITY AND HUMAN ENDEAVOR.

Native Americans regarded the Sun and Moon as indicators respectively of the active and receptive energies inherent in Nature (see p.24), as well as the measurers of time. They associated solar influences with conscious activity and the exercise of reason and the will, and lunar influences with subconscious activity and the emotional and intuitive aspects of human nature.

The Waxing Moon
This phase lasts for approximately eleven days. It is a time of growth and therefore ideal for developing new ideas and concentrating your efforts into new projects.

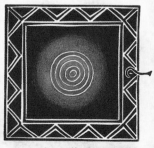

The Full Moon
Lasting about three days, this is when lunar power is at its height. It is therefore a good time for completing what was developed during the Waxing Moon.

THE FOUR PHASES

There are four phases in the twenty-nine-day lunar cycle, each one an expression of energy reflecting a particular mode of activity. They can be likened to the phases of growth of a flowering plant through the seasons: the emergence of buds (Waxing Moon), the bursting of flowers (Full Moon), the falling away of flowers (Waning Moon), and the germination of seeds (Dark Moon). The influence of each phase can be felt in two ways: in the formation of personality and in day-to-day life.

The energy expressed by the phase of the Moon at the time of your birth has a strong influence on personality. For instance, someone born during the Dark Moon is likely to be inward-looking, while a person born during the Full Moon may be more expressive. Someone born during a Waxing Moon is likely to have an outgoing nature, while a person born during a Waning Moon may be reserved. Consult a set of Moon tables to discover the phase the Moon was in on your birthday.

In your day-to-day life, the benefits of coming into harmony with the Moon's energies are considerable. Experience the energy of the four phases by consciously working with them. A Native American approach is described below.

The Waning Moon
A time for making changes, this phase lasts for an average of eleven days. Use it to improve and modify, and to dispose of what is no longer needed or wanted.

The Dark Moon
The Moon disappears from the sky for around four days. This is a time for contemplation of what has been achieved, and for germinating the seeds for the new.

THE INFLUENCE OF
ENERGY FLOW

THE MEDICINE WHEEL REFLECTS THE PERFECT BALANCE OF THE COMPLEMENTARY ACTIVE AND RECEPTIVE ENERGIES THAT COEXIST IN NATURE.

Energy flows through Nature in two complementary ways, which can be expressed in terms of active and receptive, or male and female. The active energy principle is linked with the Elements of Fire and Air, and the receptive principle with Water and Earth.

Each of the twelve birth times has an active or receptive energy related to its Elemental Aspect. Traveling around the Wheel, the two energies alternate with each birth time, resulting in an equal balance of active and receptive energies, as in Nature.

Active energy is associated with the Sun and conscious activity. Those whose birth times take this principle prefer to pursue experience. They are conceptual,

energetic, outgoing, practical, and analytical. Receptive energy is associated with the Moon and subconscious activity. Those whose birth times take this principle prefer to attract experience. They are intuitive, reflective, conserving, emotional, and nurturing.

THE WAKAN-TANKA
At the heart of the Wheel lies an S-shape within a circle, the symbol of the life-giving source of everything that comes into physical existence – seemingly out of nothing. Named by the Plains Indians as Wakan-Tanka (Great Power), it can also be perceived as energy coming into form and form reverting to energy in the unending continuity of life.

SNAKE
MEDICINE
YOUR IN-DEPTH
PERSONALITY PROFILE

SEASON OF BIRTH
FROST TIME

THE MISTY NATURE OF AUTUMN REACHES ITS PEAK IN THE SECOND BIRTH TIME OF THE SEASON, LENDING THOSE BORN THEN AN INTEREST IN THE MYSTERIOUS AND THE NEW.

Frost time is one of the twelve birth times, the fundamental division of the year into twelve seasonal segments (see pp.12–13). As the middle period of the Autumn cycle, it is the time of the year when a chill is felt in the air and the first frosts occur. Fallen leaves begin to decompose, providing the soil with nutrients in preparation for regeneration.

INFLUENCE OF NATURE
The qualities and characteristics imbued in Nature at this time form the basis of your own nature. So, just as the frozen dew hardens and seals the soil at the beginning of the day, so, if you were born during Frost time, you will often find that many of your ideas receive a frosty reception if you impart them as soon as they occur to you. Conversely, if you store your ideas – conceived by cool intellect – and allow your feelings to play over them for a while, they will evolve and solidify. Then, when you judge the climate to be warmer, if you communicate your developed ideas to others you will generally find that they are greeted with the enthusiasm they deserve.

This time of year might be compared to twilight, when light and darkness, physical and spiritual realms, overlap. To celebrate this phase, many ancient peoples held ritual bonfires on the eve of November 1, in which the problems of the year were symbolically burned. They also honored loved ones who had died, feeling their proximity during this time.

STAGE OF LIFE

This time of year might be compared to the beginning of a new phase in the middle years of life. In human development terms, it is a period of inquisitiveness and idealism, a time when life's deeper mysteries hold a special fascination. It is a time of looking at life in a new way and following unusual paths that lead to fundamental life changes. It is a time of transformation and renewed enthusiasm for living.

ACHIEVE YOUR POTENTIAL

You are full of unusual ideas and innovative schemes but often suffer disappointment in seeing them realized because you have a tendency to

Nature's energy

Nature prepares for regeneration in this, the middle cycle of Autumn. The fallen leaves blanketing the ground start to decompose, adding richness to the soil, which will need to support new growth in the Spring.

suggest them at inopportune times. In the same way, your eagerness for fresh beginnings can mean that you set off on a new path without considering whether the timing of the change is absolutely right for you and those closest to you. Try to rein back your enthusiasm for a new idea or way of life – however sound the reasons for either – in order to reflect on whether the timing for it is good. Waiting a while might well save undue frustration and suffering.

> "Life is a circle from childhood to childhood; so it is with everything where power moves." *Black Elk teaching*

27

BIRTH TOTEM
THE SNAKE

THE ESSENTIAL NATURE AND CHARACTERISTIC
BEHAVIOR OF THE SNAKE EXPRESSES THE PERSONALITY
TYPE OF THOSE BORN DURING FROST TIME.

Like the snake, people born during Frost time are purposeful, intense, inquisitive, and discerning. If you were born at this time, you have a determined, powerful nature that thrives on periodic dramatic life changes and overcoming challenges.

Ambitious and tenacious, with enormous powers of concentration, you regard obstacles in your path as spurs to the fulfillment of your dreams and aspirations, and markers in your personal development. Clear-thinking and decisive, you are not afraid to make changes to your life,

and you adapt to new circumstances with ease. You emerge from these changes transformed and renewed.

Sensuous and sensitive to others' moods and desires, you have a magnetic personality, although many find your intense, penetrating gaze unnerving. Your tendency to secrecy and keen interest in the mysterious can also be disturbing to others.

HEALTH MATTERS

Your ability to conceal deeply felt feelings and frustrations beneath a cool exterior can lead you to suffer from nervous disorders, stomach ulcers, or circulatory problems. Try to find ways to release your inner tensions.

Snake power

Regenerative and sensitive, the snake also expresses the powerful and tenacious aspects of the determined and sensuous people born at this time.

THE SNAKE AND
RELATIONSHIPS

IMAGINATIVE AND PURPOSEFUL, SNAKE PEOPLE ARE
INTRIGUING FRIENDS. THEY MAKE PASSIONATE AND LOYAL
PARTNERS BUT TEND TO HIDE THEIR FEELINGS.

With their magnetic personalities, Snake people, like their totem animal, can be hypnotic and intense creatures. If your birth totem is Snake, your determined nature and forceful energy make you a strong character, whom others look to for inspiration and leadership. However, your tendency to make dramatic changes, forging new attachments and shedding old ones, can prevent you from forming the close and trusting friendships you really need.

LOVING RELATIONSHIPS
Despite Snake people's need for constant affection, they rarely show their feelings. Male Snake is considerate but can be domineering, while female Snake is sensual and opinionated, inclined to want the

last word. Prone to extremes, both can be highly passionate lovers or occasionally celibate.

When problems arise, it is often because of your secretive nature and apparent emotional coolness, which may make your partner feel alienated and unloved. Your seriousness and intensity can also make you a less-than-relaxing companion.

COPING WITH SNAKE
Snake people are straightforward and precise, so aim for clarity and brevity in your dealings with them. Be wary of arousing their anger – they never forget a wrong. Try not to be put off by that cool facade: Snakes have deep emotions. Show them love and affection, and be patient – they have the capacity to offer great love and loyalty in return.

SNAKE IN LOVE

Snake with Falcon A volatile match. Falcons keep their feet on the ground only briefly, while Snake wants to stay there for a lifetime.

Snake with Beaver Both are intensive doers, and this is likely to be a passionate partnership to satisfy both body and mind.

Snake with Deer Snake can be considerate and caring, but Deer may find it hard to cope with Snake's intensity.

Snake with Woodpecker This could be a highly charged pairing. Each has an intensity that can divide them or create a deep bond.

Snake and Salmon Snake's intensity may undermine Salmon's ego, while Salmon's dominance may be too much for Snake. Sparks may fly.

Snake with Brown Bear They will enjoy each other's company, but Brown Bear's placidity may frustrate Snake's passionate nature.

Snake with Crow An uneasy pairing. Snake's intensity is disturbing to easygoing Crow, who prefers not to be stretched to the limit.

Snake with Snake A highly passionate relationship, but it can be undermined if one fights to control the other.

Snake with Owl These two may be physically attracted but long-term commitment will require a lot of patience and compromise.

Snake with Goose These two may not get off to a passionate start, but they can develop a strong bond and become very involved in each other's interests.

Snake with Otter Snake wants a loving relationship, while Otter is hot and cold. Both may be stubborn.

Snake with Wolf Both are sensitive, and, in spite of their differences, there is a lot going for them, so they can thrive together.

DIRECTIONAL TOTEM
THE GRIZZLY BEAR

THE GRIZZLY BEAR SYMBOLIZES THE INFLUENCE OF THE WEST ON SNAKE PEOPLE, WHO POSSESS THE ADAPTABILITY AND INNER STRENGTH TO SUCCEED.

F alling Leaves time, Frost time, and Long Nights time all fall within the quarter of the Medicine Wheel associated with the West Direction or Wind.

Grizzly bear bowl
This Tlingit wooden bowl is carved in the shape of a bear, which is associated with inner strength.

The West is aligned with Autumn and dusk, and it is associated with introspection, consolidation, maturity, and the wisdom that stems from experience. The power of the West's influence is primarily with the physical, and its principal function is the power of holding. It takes as its totem the self-sufficient grizzly bear.

The specific influence of the West on Snake people is on adaptability, enabling you to feel at ease with both material concerns and spiritual matters. The West Wind is associated with a probing intensity that can reveal hidden truths and has a strong introspective influence.

GRIZZLY CHARACTERISTICS

In Autumn, the powerful grizzly bear makes careful preparation for hibernation, storing up its inner strength for reawakening in Spring. Hence, Native Americans associated it with resourcefulness and self-reliance. It was seen as introspective because it seemed to be thoughtful about its actions; as a totem, it encourages you to look within for guidance and to learn from the past to bring wisdom to your decisions.

If your Directional totem is Grizzly Bear, you are likely to have a capacity for endurance, the resolve to face up to your weaknesses, and the courage to learn from experience.

The spirit of the West
The Sun sets in the West, symbolizing reflection; the Grizzly Bear totem signifies self-reliance.

ELEMENTAL TOTEM
THE FROG

LIKE THE FROG, WHICH IS HAPPY BOTH IN AND OUT
OF WATER, SNAKE PEOPLE'S ADAPTABLE NATURE MEANS
THEY CAN FIND SUCCESS AGAINST THE ODDS.

The Elemental Aspect of Snake people is Water. They share this Aspect with Woodpecker and Wolf people, who all therefore belong to the same Elemental family or "clan" (see pp.20–21 for an introduction to the influence of the Elements). Each Elemental clan has a totem to provide insight into its essential characteristics.

THE FROG CLAN

The totem of the Elemental clan of Water is Frog, which symbolizes a sensitive, emotional, adaptable, and intuitive nature.

The frog is at home both in water and on land, diving below the surface then sitting still, attuned to every movement around it. So, if you belong to this clan, you have the ability to adapt, while your intuition enables you to see beneath surface

Below the surface
The frog symbolizes the fundamental quality of Water: deep sensitivity.

appearances and to understand the moods of others.

Imaginative, responsive, and intense, you have deep emotions, which you "bottle up" at times. You dislike feeling vulnerable and can be secretive. Beneath your cool exterior, you crave understanding from those close to you and true freedom to express yourself both creatively and emotionally.

Water of Earth
The Element of Water feeds Earth, generating adaptability and the power of endurance.

to persist inherent in Earth. So you may sometimes find yourself in situations where your determination makes you lose sight of your own – and others' – emotional needs. This can make you feel isolated and dissatisfied, and plunge you into despair. At times like these, or when you are stressed, try the following soothing exercise. Find a quiet spot near water – with which you have a natural affinity – by a river or lake, the sea or a pool, away from the polluting effects of traffic and the activities of others.

Let the sound of the water wash over you as you breathe slowly and deeply. With each in-breath, feel the energizing power of the life force course through you, bringing you the clarity of a mountain stream, and refreshing body, mind, and spirit.

ELEMENTAL PROFILE

For Snake people, the predominant Elemental Aspect of emotional Water is affected by the qualities of your Principal Element – enduring Earth. So, if you were born at this time, you are likely to have an adaptable, resourceful personality coupled with durability, enabling you to effect transformations in your life and endure setbacks.

You may tend to be overintense and determined, driven by the turbulence of Water and the capacity

STONE AFFINITY
AMETHYST

By using the gemstone with which your own essence resonates, you can tap into the power of the Earth itself and awaken your inner strengths.

Gemstones are minerals that are formed within the Earth itself in an exceedingly slow but continuous process. Native Americans valued them not only for their beauty but also for being literally part of the Earth, and therefore possessing part of its life force. They regarded gemstones as being "alive" – channelers of energy that could be used in many ways: to heal, to protect, or for meditation.

Every gemstone has a different energy or vibration. On the Medicine Wheel, a stone is associated with each birth time, the energy of which resonates with the essence of those born during that time. Because of this energy affiliation, your stone can be used to help bring you into harmony with the Earth and to create balance within yourself. It can enhance and develop your good qualities and endow you with the qualities or abilities you need.

Faceted amethyst
The calming energy of amethyst is thought to be an aid to meditation, inspirational thought, and creativity.

ENERGY RESONANCE

Snake people have an affinity with amethyst – a crystalline quartz that ranges in color from pale violet to deep purple. Amethyst has an energy pattern that is calming and helps to restore insight and inner strength, creating a feeling of peacefulness. It was regarded by Native Americans as

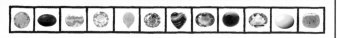

ACTIVATE YOUR GEMSTONE

Obtain a piece of amethyst and cleanse it by holding it under cold running water. Allow it to dry naturally. Then, holding the stone with both hands, bring it up to your mouth and blow into it sharply and hard, three or four times in order to impregnate it with your breath. Next, hold it firmly in one hand, and silently welcome it into your life as a friend and helper.

When you are in a stressful situation and want to access your inner wisdom, use the amethyst to help you meditate. Find a quiet spot to sit without fear of interruption and place the amethyst on your head; hold it in place with your right palm. Focus your thoughts on the stone and ask it to guide you toward a solution. Listen for the still, small voice of your inner self.

a stone that imparted the courage needed to implement change or undergo transformation. In addition, they valued it for relieving insomnia and headaches and believed it had protective properties.

Amethyst power
Wear or carry amethyst, and keep a piece in your home to promote calm.

If your birth totem is Snake, you will find amethyst especially helpful with regard to your aspirations, including spiritual concerns and creative endeavors. Its calming influence is valuable at times when you feel emotionally vulnerable or anxious, giving you a quiet inner courage and sense of tranquillity.

"The outline of the stone is round; the power of the stone is endless." Lakota Sioux teaching

TREE AFFINITY
WILLOW

GAIN A DEEPER UNDERSTANDING OF YOUR OWN NATURE
AND AWAKEN POWERS LYING DORMANT WITHIN YOU BY
RESPECTING AND CONNECTING WITH YOUR AFFINITY TREE.

Trees have an important part to play in the protection of Nature's mechanisms and in the maintenance of the Earth's atmospheric balance, which is essential for the survival of the human race.

Native Americans referred to trees as "Standing People" because they stand firm, obtaining strength from their connection with the Earth. They therefore teach us the importance of being grounded, while at the same time listening to and reaching for our higher aspirations.

When respected as living beings, trees can provide insight into the workings of Nature and our own inner selves.

On the Medicine Wheel, each birth time is associated with a particular kind of tree, the basic qualities of which complement the nature of those born during that time. Snake people have an affinity with the willow. With its long, flexible stems, the willow takes its name from an Anglo-Saxon word meaning "pliable," which is also a characteristic of the adaptable Snake. Often seen growing on riverbanks,

CONNECT WITH YOUR TREE

Appreciate the beauty of your affinity tree and study its nature carefully, for it has an affinity with your own nature.

The willow is a large, graceful tree with a thick trunk and furrowed bark. Long, narrow leaves cover its branches, and in Spring it produces both yellow and green, slender, cylindrical catkins. The willow thrives beside rivers and streams.

Try the following exercise when you need to revitalize your inner strength. Stand beside your affinity tree. Place the palms of your hands on its trunk and rest your forehead on the backs of your hands. Inhale slowly and feel energy from the tree's roots flow through your body. If easily available, obtain a cutting or twig from your affinity tree to keep as a totem or helper.

the impressive willow remains serene, in calm contrast to the surging waters below. When Snake people feel tempted to rush into things without taking time to reflect, they can tap into their own powers of inner calm by connecting with their tree (see panel above).

ADAPT AND THRIVE

If your birth totem is Snake, you are a person with intensity of purpose and great reserves of determination.

At times, however, this can make you appear obstinate; the willow, with its tenacious, spreading roots, serves to remind you of this.

Just as the willow manages to flourish in changing conditions while retaining its strong identity, so can you find the capacity to adapt to the needs of those around you without compromising your individuality. Call on the willow's help to develop your intuition, and trust your feelings more so that you act with sensitivity.

"All healing plants are given by Wakan-Tanka; therefore they are holy." Lakota Sioux teaching

COLOR AFFINITY
VIOLET

ENHANCE YOUR POSITIVE QUALITIES BY USING THE POWER OF YOUR AFFINITY COLOR TO IMPROVE YOUR EMOTIONAL AND MENTAL STATES.

Each birth time has an affinity with a particular color. This is the color that resonates best with the energies of the people born during that time, expressing their basic temperament. Exposure to your affinity color will encourage a positive emotional and mental outlook, while exposure to colors that clash with your affinity color will have a negative effect on your sense of well-being.

Violet resonates with Snake people. Made up of equal parts red and blue, it combines the influence of both these colors. Red is associated with passion and vitality, while blue suggests compassion and tranquillity, so violet is the embodiment of enthusiastic involvement,

Color scheme

Allow a violet color theme to be the thread that runs through your entire home, from the table settings and floral arrangements to the fixtures, walls, and floors.

BATHE IN YOUR COLOR

Take a bottle of lavender aromatherapy oil and add a few drops to your bath water. Gently stir the water to disperse the oil before climbing in. When you are ready, submerge your body in the water. Make sure you have at least half an hour to spare so that you can indulge in a relaxed, unhurried soaking.

Relaxing in a lavender-oil bath will release tension, relieve stress, and leave your skin feeling soft and smooth. It is especially beneficial if you are feeling emotionally drained, depressed, or are suffering from low self-esteem. Allow any thoughts and sensations to flow through your mind and body, and reflect on them as they occur.

---

sensuality, and calmness. The color of intensity and mysticism, violet suggests power and opulence. It also stimulates your perceptive and imaginative abilities and invigorates the determination and drive for success and accomplishment.

COLOR BENEFITS

Strengthen your aura and enhance your positive qualities by introducing shades of violet to the interior decor of your home.

Carefully chosen spots of color can make all the difference. A violet-tinted lampshade, for example, can alter the ambience of a room, or try filling a violet or purple vase with a bunch of lilacs or lavender.

If you need a confidence boost, try wearing something that contains violet. Whenever your energies are low, practice the color bathing exercise outlined above, to balance your emotions, awaken your creativity, and help you to feel joyful.

"The power of the spirit should be honored with its color." **Lakota Sioux teaching**

WORKING THE WHEEL
LIFE PATH

CONSIDER YOUR BIRTH PROFILE AS A STARTING POINT IN THE DEVELOPMENT OF YOUR CHARACTER AND THE ACHIEVEMENT OF PERSONAL FULFILLMENT.

ach of the twelve birth times is associated with a particular path of learning or with a collection of lessons to be learned through life. By following your path of learning, you will develop strengths in place of weaknesses, achieve a greater sense of harmony with the world, and discover inner peace.

YOUR PATH OF LEARNING
For Snake people, the first lesson in your path of learning is to cultivate

patience and flexibility in the pursuit of your dreams and the development of your ideas. Determined and purposeful, you tend to become forceful, even aggressive, when attempting to persuade others of the high value of your ideas. This approach often inspires resistance rather than acceptance in others. Try a more sensitive, less impatient stance in the future, and be

"Each man's road is shown to him within his own heart. There he sees all the truths of life." Cheyenne teaching

prepared to modify your ideas or dreams to better suit the situation of others. This should ensure a greater chance of seeing them realized.

Snake people also need to develop the inner strength required to meet the seemingly constant succession of formidable tasks that confront them. These challenges represent crucial stages of transformation in your personal development. Try not to be overwhelmed by the enormity of each task or its significance, and nurture your capacity to adapt to frequently changed circumstances.

Your third lesson is to develop more of a sense of fun. Intense and serious of purpose, you often miss out on the lighter side of life. This can make you resentful of the ability of others to enjoy themselves and unjustly critical of their light-hearted approach to life. Ensure that occasionally you take time off from the pursuit of your goals to relax.

WORKING THE WHEEL
MEDICINE POWER

HARNESS THE POWERS OF OTHER BIRTH TIMES TO
TRANSFORM YOUR WEAKNESSES INTO STRENGTHS AND
TO MEET THE CHALLENGES IN YOUR LIFE.

The whole spectrum of human qualities and abilities is represented on the Medicine Wheel. The totems and affinities associated with each birth time indicate the basic qualities with which those born at that time are equipped.

Complementary affinity
A key strength of Beaver – weak in Snake – is the ability to preserve a stable environment.

Study your path of learning (see pp.42–43) to identify those aspects of your personality that may need to be strengthened, then look at other birth times to discover the totems and affinities that can assist you in this task. For example, your Elemental profile is Water of Earth (see pp.34–35), so for balance you need the freedom and clarity of Air

and the enthusiasm of Fire. Deer's Elemental profile is Air of Fire and Falcon's is Fire of Fire, so meditate on these birth totems. In addition, you may find it useful to study the personality profiles of the other two members of your Elemental clan of Frog – Woodpecker and Wolf – to discover how the same Elemental Aspect of Water can be expressed differently.

Also helpful is the birth totem that sits opposite yours on the Medicine Wheel, which contains qualities and characteristics that complement or enhance your own. This is known as your complementary affinity, which for Snake people is Beaver.

ESSENTIAL STRENGTHS

D escribed below are the essential strengths of each birth totem. To develop a quality that is weak in yourself or that you need to meet a particular challenge, meditate upon the birth totem that contains the attribute you need. Obtain a representation of the relevant totem – a claw, tooth, or feather; a picture, ring, or model. Affirm that the power it represents is within you.

Falcon medicine is the power of keen observation and the ability to act decisively and energetically whenever action is required.

Beaver medicine is the ability to think creatively and laterally – to develop alternative ways of doing or thinking about things.

Deer medicine is characterized by sensitivity to the intentions of others and to that which might be detrimental to your well-being.

Woodpecker medicine is the ability to establish a steady rhythm throughout life and to be tenacious in protecting all that you value.

Salmon medicine is the strength to be determined and courageous in the choice of goals you want to achieve and to have enough stamina to see a task through to the end.

Brown Bear medicine is the ability to be resourceful, hardworking, and dependable in times of need, and to draw on inner strength.

Crow medicine is the ability to transform negative or nonproductive situations into positive ones and to transcend limitations.

Snake medicine is the talent to adapt easily to changes in circumstances and to manage transitional phases well.

Owl medicine is the power to see clearly during times of uncertainty and to conduct life consistently, according to long-term plans.

Goose medicine is the courage to do whatever might be necessary to protect your ideals and to adhere to your principles in life.

Otter medicine is the ability to connect with your inner child, to be innovative and idealistic, and to thoroughly enjoy the ordinary tasks and routines of everyday life.

Wolf medicine is the courage to act according to your intuition and instincts rather than your intellect, and to be compassionate.